HOW TO MAKE A BIRD WITH TWO HANDS

How to Make a Bird with Two Hands

By Mike White

WINNER OF THE 2011 WORD WORKS
WASHINGTON PRIZE

THE WORD WORKS
WASHINGTON, D.C.

FIRST EDITION   FIRST PRINTING
How to Make a Bird with Two Hands
Copyright © 2012 Mike White

Reproduction of any part of this book in any form or by any means, electronic or mechanical, except when quoted in part for the purpose of review, must be with permission from the publisher in writing. Address inquiries to:

The Word Works
PO Box 42164
Washington, DC 20015

wordworksbooks.org
editor@wordworksbooks.org

Cover art: *Bird Vision* by Stephen Snake
Author photograph: Chrisoula Andreou
Book design: Susan Pearce

Library of Congress Catalog Number: 2011938036
International Standard Book Number: 978-0-915380-81-7

ACKNOWLEDGMENTS

Grateful acknowledgment to the editors of the following magazines in which these poems first appeared, some in earlier versions:

AGNI Online: "God in the Details"; *The American Poetry Journal*: "Lascaux"; *The Antioch Review*: "Genitalia"; *Asheville Poetry Review*: "Stones" appeared as "Murder"; *Barrow Street*: "Care Instructions"; *Blink*: "O"; *Caesura*: "Flyways," "Bird in the Hand"; *Center: A Journal of the Literary Arts*: "Time Pieces"; *Cimarron Review*: "Buying My First Suit," "Kansas"; *Colorado Review*: "And"; *Columbia Poetry Review*: "Cinéma Vérité"; *Connecticut Review*: "Flo"; *Cranky Literary Journal*: "[between the equipoise of a dragonfly]"; *The Dalhousie Review*: "The Artist of Bees"; *Denver Quarterly*: "Middle Age," "Lobster Traps"; *The Evansville Review*: "Beggary"; *FIELD*: "Love"; *Fulcrum: an annual of poetry and aesthetics*: "I Am the Light"; *Gulf Coast*: "Pair"; *In Posse Review*: "Love Poem," "Second Acts"; *The Iowa Review*: "Anne Frank, Postscript," "At 18"; *MARGIE: The American Journal of Poetry*: "Bird"; *Meridian*: "Such Is the Care of the World"; *Mid-American Review*: "Butterflies," "Outer Space"; *Natural Bridge*: "Fire"; *The New Republic*: "Whale"; *Notre Dame Review*: "Power"; *Pleiades*: "Tentacled Motherfucker," "This poem is starting from where"; *Poet Lore*: "The Contortionist's Trick"; *Poetry*: "Death for Bad Guys Tastes like Candy"; *Poetry East*: "Sacrament"; *Poetry International*: "Hello"; *RATTLE*: "Bashō, Glimpsed," "NASCAR"; *River Styx*: "Attack of the Killer Dwarves"; *RUNES: A Review of Poetry*: "Hearth," "Crossing"; *Third Coast*: "Crow"; *Verse*: "Angels" appeared as "Angel," "Incarnate"; *West Branch*: "Commission," "Fitting Room," "Invitation," "Holy," "Tribe," "Wind"; *Western Humanities*

Review: "Go Around," "The Apron of the Baker," "There Was a Line She Had Crossed," "Berryman"; *Witness*: "Bridge."

"Love" was reprinted in *Poetry Daily* on April 28, 2011.

My deepest thanks to the graduate students and faculty members in the English department at the University of Utah who helped in so many ways to bring this book to fruition, and to Michael Wurster, who read my first poems and yet still encouraged me. Thank you to my entire family for their love and support, and especially to Chrisa, for everything.

FOR CHRISA AND KAEMON

CONTENTS

I

15 O
16 Wind
17 Tentacled Motherfucker
18 Buying My First Suit
19 Pair
20 Invitation
21 Bashō, Glimpsed
22 Care Instructions
23 Outer Space
24 Fitting Room
25 And
26 Flyways
27 Go Around
28 Power
29 Fire
30 Death for Bad Guys Tastes like Candy
31 Butterflies
32 Cinéma Vérité
33 God in the Details
34 Anne Frank, Postscript
35 Bird in the Hand
36 The Apron of the Baker
37 I Am the Light
38 Angels

II

41 Bridge
42 Whale
43 Berryman
44 Incarnate
45 At 18
46 Middle Age

47 Lobster Traps
48 Genitalia
49 Attack of the Killer Dwarves
51 Crow
52 NASCAR
53 Commission
54 Love Poem
55 Second Acts
56 This poem is starting from where
57 Hello
58 What Thoughts I Have of You Tonight, Frank O'Hara
59 Sacrament
60 Holy

III

63 Crossing
64 Bird
65 Love
66 Such Is the Care of the World
67 Stones
68 Time Pieces
69 There Was a Line She Had Crossed
70 [between the equipoise of a dragonfly]
71 Kansas
72 Lascaux
73 Flo
74 Touched
75 Tribe
76 The Contortionist's Trick
77 Hearth
78 The Artist of Bees
79 Beggary

81 About The Word Works
82 About the Washington Prize
83 Also from The Word Works
85 About the author / About the artist

Now, let the not become
Nothing, and so remain,
Till the bright grass birds come
Home to the singing tree.
Then, let them be.

—James Wright

I

O

begins the morning
and I have only
to wonder at this egg

white and cold
in the restful bowl
of my hand

Wind

Not a remarkable wind.
So when the bistro's patio umbrella
blew suddenly free and pitched
into the middle of the road,
it put a stop to the afternoon.

Something white and amazing
was blocking the way.

A waiter in a clean apron
appeared, not quite
certain, shielding his eyes, wary
of our rumbling engines.

He knelt in the hot road,
making two figures in white, one
leaning over the sprawled,
broken shape of the other,
creaturely, great-winged,
and now so carefully gathered in.

Tentacled Motherfucker

Lives in the sewers lives on algae lives forever

Steals mail steals checks one child still missing

Sneaks cereal bars from the Nabisco factory dumpster
(when the night guard hears rummaging out back
he puts his earphones on and loudly hums)

Once an uncanny shadow under a bridge
identified by two boys sniffing paint thinner

Makes a moaning sound makes a sobbing sound

Rings the church bell at unlikely hours

Starts weird fires and the sky turns green

Paints ravishing nocturnal murals

In the railroad yard there's a little vegetable garden
no one remembers planting

Buying My First Suit

I remember thinking
how I had grown

too few hands
to fill the outer
and the inner pockets.

Then, as instructed,
I checked the pockets.
Hands.

Pair

Go find your mother's legs
was like
Go clean your room.

Except you had no room.
That was the difference.

The room you didn't have
was one place
they would not be.

That was how things
could be seen.

You had no toys.
They were made of wood.

Invitation

To the boy not me
who drowned
in the swollen river
and who returned
for a month of nights
riding my borrowed bike

I say come again come
inside and get warm

now we are older
the river is dry
let us put aside our differences

Bashō, Glimpsed

miles from
anywhere, NV

head down
walking

        nothing
on his back

but the moon

Care Instructions

I am happy in the days
following my routine
self-exam

to come across
another man's raincoat.

Listen: it's reversible.

The way I was at his age.
The way he was at mine.

To wash it
you must step outside
continually, continually.

Outer Space

And it is difficult
to get abducted
even in a cornfield.

You remind yourself again
how it took every ounce
of luck just to be born.

*We have been
expecting you*
they always say.

You are like them,
obsessed with secrecy
and perfect circles.

They are interested.
Go on, they say, nodding
in unison like sunflowers.

It is the inner space
that hurts most, you say,
the not knowing.

But by now the translator
is preoccupied,
fiddling at the controls.

Fitting Room

I met my old spiritual mentor in the mirror.
He looked just like my doubles partner.
It was uncanny. I was
unprepared. "Aren't you . . ."
he began, raising an incredulous finger.

And

      bringing the sky

to bear
      on our conversation

           you pointed, and

the pigeons
      scattered in

      countless blue directions

Flyways

> "I am nature."
> —*Jackson Pollock*

A migrant day laborer
in Utah reported
seeing the brightest bird
in all of Mexico.

Diagnosed with a rare
incurable disease she
discovered an astonishing
new vocabulary.

He dropped his shovel
finding he needed both
hands to describe the color.

A Pollock
of words she grew
fluent and died.

Go Around

Happiness may not be communicable.
Yet there are cables under the ground.
Have you seen the men digging?
This one shoulders a section of pipe.
That one is directing traffic.
Go around his arm says.
It is late afternoon and wavy hot.
He has forgotten his arm
is connected to his body.
Here was once a seashore.
Here was once a dinosaur.
There is a tiny horse in the concrete.
There is a brain we share.

Power

Thinking of Li Po
in exile   severed

from the known world   his

lone lamp dark
thoughts thickening

I call the utility company
and a voice says

We know you
are without power
Do not touch that line

kindred a moment
with moon and shadow

he raises a cup of wine
in a nameless place
1300 years ago

Fire

or whatever's up there
sweet-talking the moon
through its phases of engorgement

must also be what's licking
the doughy electrical
mass of the arsonist's brain

as he solemnly kneels
in a Red Roof Inn boiler room
above a tinder pile of Gideon Bibles

watching amazed his own candescent hands
describe a pair of moths working
and working the charge in the dark.

Death for Bad Guys Tastes like Candy

which explains why there's no hurrying
the bad guy when he's got the good
guy right where he wants him
sweating under the industrial saw blade
that advances so slowly you wonder
how such a speed setting could ever be
useful in the manufacture of anything
though it's just the thing for the bad
guy who lives to savor the almost
unbearable anticipatory sweetness of
death drawn out to an eternity
of close-ups alternating between two men
(every pipe in the place is steaming) who share
a certain moral fanaticism and a passion
for the pretty office girl turned militia-queen
who is just now regaining consciousness
and taking her cue from the swelling
music is maneuvering a giant meathook
onto a giant pendulum and still the bad guy
has time to finish the good guy with the flick
of a switch but he chooses instead to method-
ically turn and take the meathook full on
with a slo-mo grimace and a long tapering moan
that always means a happy ending

Butterflies

No one will read to the end of a poem about butterflies.
Better to begin with the moths. The story of how
they fed on your dead neighbor
and carried him off in subatomic morsels
until there was no trace left of him.
No dental records. No nothing.
The case is not standard. For one thing
the rate of decomposition in a man eaten by moths
is typically slowed by a factor of 10.
Never mind. Facts run parallel in a poem.
Draw our attention gently back
to the moths in the living room hovering
above the crackling radio like they think
the war is still on. *We* would naturally
gravitate toward the man rotting on the ottoman
and get no further. But a moth is different.
A moth will contentedly sit
on the lip of a teacup for days
surveying the quiet wreckage of a widower's pantry.
These details need to be established early on in the poem
so that when the butterflies complete the perfect picnic
and the lovers fuck in the forest
we at least have some context.

Cinéma Vérité

The rain is reserved
for love in the movies.

Yesterday I met
two famous practitioners

under one umbrella, running
through neon puddles

past the director's cut,
a yellow cab door opening.

God in the Details

I've seen to it that ants
carry their dead

in the ceremonial style
of a great long poem

but the distances
are manageable

and how heavy
after all is an ant

when I am myself
a shadow borne

so lightly

Anne Frank, Postscript

I caught my death
in the winter of the year,
when the fresh snow was falling
I caught it, amazed,
on the tip of my tongue.

Bird in the Hand

Make it a live bird
wing-shattered and gasping
in a storm drain

and such a hand
as could conceivably hold
the flutter behind those bones.

The Apron of the Baker

When no one was looking
and the baker asleep
on his callused feet,
doused in flour, pale
as a movie corpse,
an angel came through
the delivery door
and wrapped its gentle
celestial body around
his body, a miracle
or something
holding something else
at bay, the colorless
slabs of dough rising
unbidden in his brain,
row upon row,
row upon row,
and the loaves falling out
black beyond hope.

I Am the Light

What, my lord, is a moth?

A white shadow
on a crust of spring snow.

A lesser dove
who comes when you call.

Angels

Do you hear? Does anyone
hear the man
repeating and repeating
himself in the snow?

II

Bridge

A man shouting
from the guardrail

I have no wings
I have no wings
I have no wings

In my America
he keeps shouting

Whale

In one version of events
Jonah was swallowed
by the whale
nightly and each morning
he recounted his story.

Jonah was shut
in a windowless room and instructed
to draw his whale.

The instructor was kind.
This was no age of monsters.

In one version of events
Jonah put thumbtacks
in his eyes
and sounded the room's
shadowy circumference.

Berryman

who the water bore

in a slow dream

borne John Smith

an everyman

Henry made

of bits of paper

the water bore

hymning himself

an Orpheus or

a buoyant Ophelia

mad for love

and restitution

Incarnate

Dreaming the ghost not given.

I do not say wishing.

(The angel he listens.)

Does a god grow?

And kick?

Which way to pray?

I swallow stones by the river.

I lie down and cry myself ordinary.

My husband calls in his sleep *Mary, Mary.*

At 18

I was a minor god
who could create
a canopy of stars

by killing the lights
as the car sped me softly
into whatever and the dark.

Middle Age

for Frank O'Hara, who never had one

Look out! it's springtime in midtown
and everywhere you turn grown
men in loft apartments are falling
over themselves flowerpot-sniffing.
Grown men! show me one.
I am in the business of debunking.
Here is my card.
Here is my wallet.
Here is my pants.
In the back pocket you will find
an edible self-portrait.
I've started it
but feel free . . .
In order to buy myself time
I shout over my shoulder
*Is that Georgia O'Keeffe I see
over there painting vaginas?*
We are in a race to find out.
He shouts *The child is father
of the man* and just like that
he's leapfrogged over me.
I get lost in interpretation and wonder
if it is my father or my son
running away so fast with my pants on.

Lobster Traps

She came inside using the latest technology.
How was your day?
The bird in the clock talking.
She couldn't recall
what kind of bird exactly but turquoise and exotic.
There once had been a parrot
that chewed through her mail-order catalogs
and then her thesis.
One day it made a nasty hole in a man's hand.
It was destroyed.
Do you have any idea
just how long this species lives?
The vet had asked that question
semi-rhetorically she thought.
Back at the pet store
with her merchandise and original receipt
left-behind signs in the window
announced *Sale* and *Neutered*
and the jumble of cages on the sidewalk
reminded her suddenly of lobster traps and that
summer in Maine.

Genitalia

Like money more or less
since you can't fan your wad in public
nowadays unless as mom
said you're prepared to lose it

and look how the animals are rich
in so many senses
since they can sniff a crotch
at close quarters or at a hundred paces
without even dreaming up dirty names

which are pseudonyms we use
in our intimate correspondences
with ourselves mostly and notice how only
the luckiest in life have pet names
bestowed on what it is we share
in the dark and tender middle of things.

Attack of the Killer Dwarves

One of the early and now largely
neglected Japanese sci-fi films
features a breed of sinister bonsai trees
that decimates bustling post-war Tokyo.
The trees are the brainchild of an evil
botanist who (we are told in monotone
voiceover) had been unpopular as a boy.
Naturally he rears his bonsai
in his own stunted image. They respond
sluggishly at first to his paternal counsel to
kill, kill, my little darlings.
But practice makes perfect and in no time
his assiduous pruning results
in a perfected race of remorseless miniatures.
Thirty minutes in, at the crucial turning
point when the bonsai are set
to awaken from their long vegetative slumber
into a life of mass slaughter,
the budget runs out—
the next scene, the last scene, no less
than three hours long, comprises one continuous reel
of blotchy archival footage.
Dresden, Rotterdam, Warsaw, Hiroshima.
Tokyo becomes all
of them, becomes an unrecognizable

and undifferentiated necropolis
of toppled buildings, bodies,
white ash.
As the theater is now almost empty
we must keep reminding ourselves, we
the true believers, creatures
of imagination, that the unseen
killers are only bonsai,
that this is all just
someone's idea of a joke.

Crow

is our risible
rooster of evening

laughing it up
atop the refuse heap.

I am coming down
with something

as surely
as you are.

Crow hangs out
in back of the hospital

where the orderlies
flirt with the nurses.

As a symbol
crow is all

but extinct.
He lives on

cigarette butts
and medical waste.

Caw caw.
Wink wink.

NASCAR

Not rolling in liquid fire
or pulled apart by physics.
Not between commercials.

But the way an old dog
half-blind
noses around and around

some quiet
apple-scented
chosen ground.

Commission

Death is painting *Nocturne in Black Monochrome*
upon the domed ceiling of my skull.
This is not art, I know as much, but Death . . .

who am I to tell Death to go home,
who shows up every day at dawn
with rumpled smock and empty hands?

Love Poem

The way people get killed by the Mob
that is how we love.

It is the late night pick-up
and then the long slow drive in the country.

It is my head lying across your torso
in the baroque interior of a black sedan.

It is the beautiful and accidental shape we make
after years in the soft swale of the riverbed.

It is never being discovered.
Not by half.

Second Acts

> "There are no second acts in American lives."
> —*F. Scott Fitzgerald*

The handcuffed starlet
performing an awkward
backward self-embrace.

The social critic gesticulating
in a public library bathroom stall.
"What does *this* say about *us*?"

The glassy-eyed cyclist-turned-
analyst recalling how in the Pyrenees
he could always dream away his legs.

The swing vote in the jury box
itching for forty years
in the place a landmine dispatched.

This poem is starting from where

the last one left off. I wasn't alive
to the last one. I wanted to believe I was
the woman pushing the dead baby
in the stroller. But now I see
that our situations could not have been
more different. The poor woman
was in the dark all along, trundling
death like a cosseted bomb; while I,

I was busily rigging the circling birds
into tercets. Really, what kind of man
puts a dead baby in a stroller?
If this poem cannot revoke the last,
let me at least walk beside the woman
and gently take her hand,
a childless stranger, like Whitman
in his self-returning Song.

Hello

Thinking of all the lives
I've missed, living this one,
I halve,
then quarter
the shiny red apple.

I even thought
to use a plate
as you, my bee, would have done.

What Thoughts I Have of You Tonight, Frank O'Hara

There are no more poems
and he is not the same
man only in baggier clothes
he has gone through changes
like the city he loves
almost completely blind
he thinks about paintings
he says he would like to check
sometimes a color
and clouds he says smiling
I never noticed them before
anyway they mean rain
so we go to the movies
where he gets a discount
and talks through the plot
about famous people
he knew at one time
which for Frank is now
do you see
he says suddenly *that beautiful face*
reaching a hand in the dark
and he is clean
as any old man

Sacrament

What were we saying?
Right, you were talking
and I was listening

intently more or less when
the semi overturned
and so many cows suddenly

it was India
if it was anything

and you
were saying for
what seemed like forever

your marriage
or your wife's marriage

and I was nodding yes
you got that right
it's just the way you say

while those cows
over your left shoulder

made everyone slow down,
mouths full of roadside flowers.

Holy

Be always
on the make.

Everything comes
word of mouth.

Seek the berry
in the bear shit.

Shirt-shine it
brother.

III

Crossing

Driving through the greener suburbs, my brain
full of stops, I came upon a yellow sign
announcing, pictorially, that just ahead
was a duck crossing.
                              You can't imagine
my sudden happiness, to be reminded
simply of ducks, that ducks are with us,

and what's more, that they might, this very moment,
duckwalk single file across my path, that I
would need to yield, use unusual care.
What else makes a person
turn off the radio and quack the rest of the way home?

Bird

The brain-sick bird
has drawn a small crowd.

On the sidewalk, unafraid
of passing feet, the bird pivots
and turns and turns, unsteady
wings outstretched
in some old dream of flight.

On and on without end or interruption
until someone gasps out laughing.

Love

He says he saw a moose once.
She disagrees.

The letters they exchanged in the war
molder in the attic.

There is a chemical process that describes
why they are unreadable.

Such Is the Care of the World

You are not even required to leave
a note saying the extra key is
in the flowerbed

wrapped in tinfoil
in the proximity of the rosebush.

Stones

The most torn angel
came into town and
we were dazzled
and a little afraid

His one shredded wing he held
to his side like a secret
and for all our asking
he would not speak of God

An angel fully broken
so that when we finally
led him up the road
(gathering stones as we did)

He trusted us
like a serious child
and asked again for nothing
but water and homecoming

Time Pieces

They counseled patience
waiting for the tide
to wash him back in

―――

He'd set his watch
carefully on the night table

―――

Days or years lugging around
that great mahogany suitcase of his

―――

Quit worrying he'd say
I'm not going to be
gone a minute

There Was a Line She Had Crossed

then there was the line she was becoming

in her wild protracted dreams thinning into

God or a contrail of airplane bisecting

the homogenous winter sky at dusk a moment

then a moment longer

between the equipoise of a dragonfly

———————————

and the needle in the swimming pool

Kansas

What I crave:
the restful eye, just one
unspinning place
from which to watch
the elegant grandstand shudder,
totter, and plunge headlong

into the storm, finding the most
surprising elephantine grace
tumbling in perfect freedom
across the baseball diamond
before splintering
into unforeseeable configurations.

Lascaux

When the hunter woke before dawn
to a low fire and the old abysmal damp,
did his tired eyes linger
on his ochre-painted walls,
the herd forever galloping and forever

stilled amid a torrent of enchanted spears?
And did his heart grow sick
at the prospect of another day
in breathless pursuit
of those long ungovernable strides?

Flo

I am fed through a tube.
Soon it will get dark.
I lie still
and everything moves
in my direction.

Touched

There is a man who can manipulate clouds,
like balloons into animals, with his mind.

He lives alone, in Iowa,
so there is no one to notice
but livestock,
and they don't, particularly.

Sixty, seventy years of corn
touched by wind
in the charcoal of evening,
with insects.

Here he is.

He has just cut the motor
on his green tractor,
his body still
humming with the movement,
his ears the sound,
raising his wide hands to the sky.

It is a life people like me
contemplate from airplanes.

We can see that far, right
down to the man squinting up
from the seat of his green tractor,
adjusting and adjusting.

Tribe

No one lives anywhere
but in these mountains.
And it is so
beautiful and difficult
to live in these mountains.

The Contortionist's Trick

Say there is a box
that can accommodate
half a person

just say

and crawl inside

the work
of a lifetime

Hearth

A bird has flown
down the chimney.
A redbird, a fistful
of molten life.

We once made space
for such luck.
Roused
from coiled dreams

we'd beat the pans
till daybreak,
then raise a fable
from the common ash.

The Artist of Bees

Kind of you to put it
that way. Truer to say
I own an acre of clover
and the bees come and go
much as they please. Still
once I was bearded
with bees and someone
took a picture. My art
is now the spumy cloud
you can see there in the trees.
There is no talking down bees.
Let us sit and wait,
you and I, here
in the buzzing shade.

Beggary

To peel an orange
by its own light

is to make nothing
happen

and the scent of orange
on my hands

that is nothing
as well

ABOUT THE WORD WORKS

The Word Works, a nonprofit literary organization, publishes contemporary poetry collections and presents public programs. Since 1981, the organization has sponsored the Washington Prize, a monetary award and book publication for an American or Canadian poet. Monthly, The Word Works offers free literary programs in the Chevy Chase, MD, Café Muse series, and each summer, it holds free poetry programs in Washington, DC's Rock Creek Park. Annually in June, two high school students debut in the Joaquin Miller Series as winners of the Jacklyn Potter Young Poets Competition. Other programs have included workshops, master classes, symposia, international artist retreats, panel discussions, and archival projects with prominent American poets.

As a 501(c)3 organization, The Word Works has received awards from the National Endowment for the Arts, National Endowment for the Humanities, DC Commission on the Arts & Humanities, Witter Bynner Foundation, Poets & Writers, The Writer's Center, Bell Atlantic, the David G. Taft Foundation, and others, including many generous private patrons. The Word Works has established an archive of artistic and administrative materials in the Washington Writing Archive housed in the George Washington University Gelman Library. The Word Works is a member of the Council of Literary Magazines and Presses and distributed by Small Press Distribution.

More information at wordworksbooks.org.

ABOUT THE WASHINGTON PRIZE

How to Make a Bird with Two Hands is the winner of the 2011 Word Works Washington Prize. Mike White's collection was selected from among 327 manuscripts submitted by American and Canadian poets.

FIRST READERS: Barbara Anderson • Stuart Bartow Wendy Chin-Tanner • George Drew • Peter Fernbach Michelle Galo • Joshua Gray • Elaine Handley • Erich Hintz Diane Lockward • Amy MacLennan • Marilyn McCabe Kathleen McCoy • Miles David Moore • Yvonne Murphy Danielle Pierratti

SECOND READERS: Karren Alenier • Brad Richard • Jay Rogoff Barbara Louise Ungar

FINAL JUDGES: J. H. Beall • Leslie McGrath • Margo Stever Nancy White • Maria van Beuren

OTHER WASHINGTON PRIZE BOOKS

Nathalie F. Anderson, *Following Fred Astaire*, 1998
Michael Atkinson, *One Hundred Children Waiting for a Train*, 2001
Carrie Bennett, *biography of water*, 2004
Peter Blair, *Last Heat*, 1999
Richard Carr, *Ace*, 2008
Ann Rae Jonas, *A Diamond Is Hard but Not Tough*, 1997
Frannie Lindsay, *Mayweed*, 2009
Richard Lyons, *Fleur Carnivore*, 2005
Fred Marchant, *Tipping Point*, 1993, 3rd printing 1999
Ron Mohring, *Survivable World*, 2003
Brad Richard, *Motion Studies*, 2010
Jay Rogoff, *The Cutoff*, 1994
Prartho Sereno, *Call from Paris*, 2007
Enid Shomer, *Stalking the Florida Panther*, 1987, 2nd printing 1993
John Surowiecki, *The Hat City after Men Stopped Wearing Hats*, 2006
Miles Waggener, *Phoenix Suites*, 2002
Nancy White, *Sun, Moon, Salt*, 1992, 2nd edition 2010

ALSO FROM THE WORD WORKS

FROM THE HILARY THAM CAPITAL COLLECTION

Mel Belin, *Flesh That Was Chrysalis*
Doris Brody, *Judging the Distance*
Sarah Browning, *Whiskey in the Garden of Eden*
Grace Cavalieri, *Pine Crest Rest Home*
Christopher Conlon, *Gilbert and Garbo in Love*
   Mary Falls: Requiem for Mrs. Surratt
Donna Denizé, *Broken like Job*
W. Perry Epes, *Nothing Happened*
James Hopkins, *Eight Pale Women*
Brandon Johnson, *Love's Skin*
Marilyn McCabe, *Perpetual Motion*
Judith McCombs, *The Habit of Fire*
Miles David Moore, *The Bears of Paris*
   Rollercoaster
Kathi Morrison-Taylor, *By the Nest*
Maria Terrone, *The Bodies We Were Loaned*
Hilary Tham, *Bad Names for Women*
   Counting
Barbara Ungar, *Charlotte Brontë, You Ruined My Life*
Jonathan Vaile, *Blue Cowboy*
Rosemary Winslow, *Green Bodies*
Michele Wolf, *Immersion*

INTERNATIONAL EDITIONS

Yoko Danno & James C. Hopkins, *The Blue Door*
Moshe Dor, Barbara Goldberg, Giora Leshem, eds.,
   The Stones Remember
Moshe Dor (Barbara Goldberg, trans.), *Scorched by the Sun*
Myong-Hee Kim, *Crow's Eye View: The Infamy of Lee Sang,*
   Korean Poet
Vladimir Levchev, *Black Book of the Endangered Species*

ADDITIONAL TITLES

Karren L. Alenier, *Wandering on the Outside*
Karren L. Alenier, Hilary Tham, Miles David Moore, eds.,
   Winners: A Retrospective of the Washington Prize
Christopher Bursk, *Cool Fire*
Barbara Golderg, *Berta Broadfoot and Pepin the Short*
Jacklyn Potter, Dwaine Rieves, Gary Stein, eds., *Cabin Fever:*
   Poets at Joaquin Miller's Cabin
Robert Sargent, *Aspects of a Southern Story*
   A Woman from Memphis

ABOUT THE AUTHOR

Mike White grew up in Montreal, and lived in Canada until 2001. With a Bachelor's degree from The University of Toronto and a Masters from McGill University, he headed south to the University of Utah's doctoral program in Literature and Creative Writing. He served as the poetry editor and editor-in-chief of *Quarterly West* and teaches literature and creative writing courses at the University of Utah.

His poems have appeared in *Poetry*, *The New Republic*, *The Threepenny Review*, *The Iowa Review*, *The Antioch Review*, *FIELD*, *Witness*, and many others. Work has also been featured online at *Poetry Daily* and *Verse Daily*. He maintains ties with the Canadian literary scene, with poems in Canadian journals such as *The Malahat Review*, *The Dalhousie Review*, and *The Fiddlehead*.

How to Make a Bird with Two Hands is his first book.

ABOUT THE ARTIST

Stephen Snake was born on the Rama Ojibway Reserve near Orillia, Ontario, in 1966. A natural born artist, Stephen's gift was recognized and supported by his artist mother Carol Shilling. Arthur Shilling, a cousin of Carol's, became a strong influence on Stephen's direction as an artist. Now, Stephen's art is shown throughout the world. Stephen lives on Lake Temagami where he paints landscapes, portraits and woodland styles of work using oil and acrylic. Stephen continues to capture and illustrate the spiritual and mystical nature of Temagami's rocks, water, and trees.

www.ingramcontent.com/pod-product-compliance
Lightning Source LLC
Chambersburg PA
CBHW020950090426
42736CB00010B/1348